# BEEN THERE AND BACK AGAIN

## Why I said good-bye to holiness standards

**Sylvia Brown**

Printed in the United States of America

Sylvia Brown
P.O. Box 4424
South Bend, IN 46634
bookbeenthereandback@gmail.com

ISBN 978-1-365-92225-1

*To Danielle, David, and Ricky*
*III John 4*
*"I have no greater joy than to hear that my children walk in truth."*

*This page intentionally left blank.*

Dear Reader,

First and foremost, I give thanks to the Almighty God for all that He has done and what He is still doing in my life. I am not perfect and I don't pretend to have all the answers. I am also not trying to offend anyone with this book. This is simply my testimony. Some who read this book will strongly disagree with what I have to say. I ask only that you read the book to the end, and if what I have shared causes you to ponder even just a little bit, then I have done what I intended to do. It is not important to me that we all agree, but it is important for me to share because this is my praise to God for what He has done for me, and with me, in my own journey.

May God bless each person who takes the time to read what I have written.

*Sylvia Brown*

*This page intentionally left blank.*

# HOLINESS UNTO THE LORD

***To the natural Jews, chosen people of God:***

For thou art a holy people unto the Lord thy God: the Lord thy God hath chosen thee to be a special people unto himself, above all people that are upon the face of the earth.

Deuteronomy 7:6

And they shall call them, The holy people,
The redeemed of the Lord.

Isaiah 62:12

***To the spiritual Jews, chosen people of God:***

But ye are a chosen generation, a royal priesthood, a holy nation, a peculiar people; that ye should shew forth the praises of him who hath called you out of darkness into his marvellous light.

I Peter 2:9

Follow peace with all men, and holiness, without which no man shall see the Lord."

Hebrews 12:14

*This page intentionally left blank.*

# TABLE OF CONTENTS

| | |
|---|---|
| It's Been A Long time Coming | 11 |
| Change Was On The Way | 15 |
| Been There, Done That | 20 |
| Back To The Beginning | 27 |
| Who Invented Holiness Anyway? | 37 |
| 21st Century Relevance | 42 |
| The Debate | 53 |
| It's Personal | 60 |
| Legalism | 65 |
| Keeping It Real For the Ladies | 74 |
| Lessons From The Journey | 81 |

*This page intentionally left blank.*

# IT'S BEEN A LONG TIME COMING

This is my story. It's not anyone else's. I tell this story as my testimony of what God has brought me through. It's not intended to be an argument or a point for the liberal or the conservative or for any other purpose other than giving God glory. This is my story about why I decided to abandon the holiness teachings about clothing standards and begin wearing makeup, jewelry, and pants.

I was not raised in an apostolic household. I am not $10^{th}$ generation or umpteenth generation or anything like that. I found God when I was twelve years old, got baptized in Jesus' name when I was thirteen, and received the baptism of the Holy Ghost when I was fourteen. Really, I should say that God found me. Because I really wasn't looking for God, but God was looking for me. My life was that of a normal teenager. I wasn't a bad person, but I also wasn't overly concerned with spiritual things.

I want to also make it clear that my relationship with God is a personal thing. It's personal because it's not based on what someone else thinks about me or my beliefs. What God has done in my life, no church or organization or affiliation could have done that. His peace and joy that I experience in my heart does not come from my association with a particular church and is not a result of anything that I could have done.

So, here's what happened: when I was just in my early teens, I started attending a conservative apostolic church, a church that believed that Christians should be modest or conservative and that there should be gender distinction in clothing choices. The women of these churches wore dresses or skirts, did not wear sleeveless tops, did not wear jewelry except maybe a wedding or engagement ring, did not wear unnecessary cosmetics – they might use some face cream or lip balm - and did not wear any clothing that showed thighs, cleavage, or shoulders. There were guidelines for the men also, but as this is my story, and I am female, I focus only on the part that applied to me.

For the first fifteen years or so after becoming an apostolic, I wore only dresses and skirts, no makeup, no ornamental jewelry, and chose outfits that were conservative. I embraced this modest lifestyle for reasons that I will explain later.

Please bear in mind that my parents were not, and are still not, apostolics. Although I faced ridicule for my choice, the choice was entirely mine. I think everyone - from family members to well-meaning friends to complete strangers - at one time or another made comments about my choices. But, I had no interest in bearing my bosom or showing off my legs, even as a vibrant young woman, with a to-die-for 21-inch waist.

This continued even after high school when I attended a large "party school" university far away from home. Sometimes I was the only skirt-wearer in the crowd. I was completely comfortable with that. I loved it when someone asked me about my skirts. I saw it as an opportunity to witness. I was not intimidated in any way. And I held to my convictions long after I completed undergraduate college and moved on with my life and career. It wasn't always easy, but I held on, secure in my convictions.

But then things began to change. The convictions I held dear for so long became challenging like never before. Not only were my convictions unpopular among unbelievers, but some believers were also raising more and more questions about holiness standards. By the time I entered grad school a few years later, the climate was just right for a change.

## CHANGE WAS ON THE WAY

My life began to change and my convictions began to unravel. I decided to return to school for my doctorate, and the school I attended was in Michigan. Michigan - the place where I am convinced ice and snow was created. Depending on where you live, it's cold in September. And it's cold in May. Unless you have been in extreme northern temperatures, it is difficult to understand the depth of cold climate that occurs in these parts. I remember wearing jeans, with long johns, with a long wool coat, and still feeling frozen just to walk a few blocks from my car to the building. Trust me when I say that it was brutal.

With the near frostbite, I slowly began to have a change of heart. My convictions were no longer convenient for my circumstances, and I began to question my beliefs. So, I started wearing jeans only when I was at school, convincing myself that it was a necessity. Soon, I was wearing jeans all the time at school regardless of the weather. In time, I hardly thought about what I was wearing anymore. I admit that it was easier not to have to think about it. It seemed to me a type of freedom to be able to wear what I wanted wherever I wanted.

Other people's opinions, which were freely shared, caused me to question whether conservative clothing was even really required. In Michigan, I was among new friends, and even a new church environment. While it had not bothered me during my undergraduate years, for some reason the remarks about my clothing choices and no makeup bothered me during my graduate school years. I was a new face in a new place and it was important for me to make friends. In addition, law school is extremely difficult. I needed the camaraderie of my fellow law students, and I felt that the easiest way to fit in would be to look like everyone else.

The third thing that affected my decision to change my clothing standard was the fashion trends at the time. It was just easier to walk into a store – any store – and be able to find something to wear. No longer did I have to examine an outfit to see whether it was long enough or too sheer or anything else. And, let's face it, skirts and dresses are expensive. So, my pocketbook rejoiced also.

By the time I graduated from law school, I had a closet full of jeans and sweatshirts, but I was still wearing skirts to church, so I had a nice balance. But then, I began shopping for those lovely dark suits that I would need for interviews and new employment. To my dismay, the fashion trend at the time – or maybe it was just the stores in the town where I lived – favored mostly pant suits. It was very, very difficult to find skirt suits at the time. The only available skirt suits were those with skirts that were too short or that were too expensive for my budget. So, I eventually settled for pants suits, and before I knew it, I had a closet full of jeans, sweatshirts, and pant suits. The only remaining skirts in my closet were those I wore to church.

Shortly afterwards, I relocated to another state for a new job. All those dark suits paid off to a lovely job in my field. So, I started attending a new, more liberal, church. Like many apostolic churches today, this church held fast to the oneness doctrine, but was flexible with clothing standards. Attending a church that did not have the clothing standards made it easier for me to just give in altogether.

Once I began wearing pants suits on a daily basis, the rest was a slippery slope. If I was going all the way out to impress my new employers and those around me, I figured I might as well add the makeup and a little jewelry. Soon, I was regularly wearing all of the above, and in some cases did not consider myself fully dressed until I had applied at least foundation, eyeshadow, and lipstick. It didn't matter, I reasoned. My new church didn't care either way.

So, for the next 15 years, I dressed the part. Before I knew it, I had more pants than dresses in my closet. It was just something that happened over time. It was definitely easier and more economical to pick whatever was on the rack without thinking about standards.

I never went overboard, however. I wore makeup tastefully and wore only a modest amount of jewelry. Still, for someone who used to wear no jewelry, I now had a jewelry box, so the change was definitely significant. For someone who used to wear no makeup, I now had a drawer in my bathroom dedicated to just makeup – different colors of eye shadow, lipstick, nail polish, and makeup brushes.

It might be difficult for someone who has never "crossed over" to understand. The world as we know it wears makeup each and every day. Most women - and perhaps a few men - wear at least some makeup on a regular basis. Most women wear jewelry. To the modern world there is no such thing as a woman who does not enjoy jewelry: Diamonds are a girl's best friend. Pants have become so popular that some women do not even own skirts, and purchase skirts only for special occasions. So, in that sense I relate to Dinah, who was just simply a girl who was trying to fit in with the other girls.

So I made a choice to fit in. I embraced what other apostolics seemed to be doing anyway. It was easier than being different.

## BEEN THERE, DONE THAT

Everything about changing made sense to me at the time, and I developed pat excuses for anyone who asked. When I was in graduate school, it was the weather. When I moved for a new job, skirt suits were too expensive. When I got settled in my job, I wanted to fit in. Later on, I used the excuse of convenience. At each phase I defended my choices, and was quick to point out that "everyone" was doing it.

Despite all this, I never stopped living for God. I was never completely comfortable with my new "no standards" lifestyle, but since everyone else was doing it, I stifled my conscience. But my values and my desire to live for God remained the same. I still attended an apostolic church, albeit one that was lenient on clothing standards. I still believed Acts 2:38 and John chapter 3 where Jesus said we must be born again. I still spoke in tongues. I still worshipped God with all my heart and continued to feel the presence of God. It is important for me to point this out because I want those that read my testimony to understand that this was an issue about standards and nothing else.

Besides all that, many apostolic organizations are now rethinking the holiness standards issue. Some of the major organizations no longer teach on holiness standards. They say that teaching about holiness standards is really legalism and they want no part of it. Revival is happening like never before. Just like Joel prophesied in Joel chapter 2, the Holy Ghost is being poured out on a plethora of people. Millions of people from every denomination and walk of life have been baptized in the Spirit. People are coming to God from different backgrounds where they were not taught to dress a certain way, and they are very reluctant to change. Others who were raised in such teachings have chosen to understate those issues and focus on topics for victorious living. I recently spoke with a pastor of a church who said that although she personally wore only skirts and still believed the holiness teachings, she did not feel comfortable asking members of her congregation to do the same. So, given that many Holy Ghost filled people are now wearing earrings down to their shoulders and speaking in tongues with lipstick and eyeshadow, I thought all was well. Any discomfort I had was placed on the proverbial back burner and I did in Rome as the Romans do.

But, then God began dealing with my heart a little more. Since I wasn't attending a church where this mattered, I knew that it was not coming from man. If standards had been something crammed down my throat by a preacher or a parent, I probably would have shrugged it off as many do. I would have blamed the church for being oppressive, or I might have declared it to be legalism. But that wasn't the case. The church I attended was open to different interpretations about holiness and clothing standards.

But I knew what God had placed in my heart back in the beginning, and I knew that God was again speaking to my heart. I agonized over this because I wanted to please God, but my flesh wasn't really that willing to give up what I had. No one was making me dress one way or the other, so I lingered over my decision.

I wish I could say that I was obedient enough to make an instantaneous decision. I wasn't. I wrestled with the decision for about a year and a half. I reasoned that many respected people who I believed to be anointed did not feel that dress standards were important. I reasoned that everyone else in my profession was doing it, and that it was important for me to fit in with my professional community. I was fearful that my colleagues would notice the change and worried that it would have a negative impact. I was still attending the same church and did not feel like God was leading me to leave, so I knew it might be awkward. Basically, I was looking for a loophole.

Plus, I *had* been obedient about a bunch of other things that God asked me to do. I was a Sunday school teacher and a door-knocker. I was faithful in prayer and fasting. I did whatever the pastor asked me to do and then some. I gave my money and my time. I still felt the presence of God, with or without earrings. Wasn't those things enough?

I wrestled over and over with my conscience. I knew that God loved me just the way I was. I knew that He is a merciful God so I wasn't worried about some kind of doomsday coming down on my head or anything like that. I fasted. I prayed. I really sought God for an easier way or for permission to do it my way. I also knew that God required obedience. The bottom line was that I needed to be obedient.

Finally, I submitted to God. After much thought and prayer, I said yes to God's will for my life. I made the decision to forego pants, makeup, and jewelry. After fifteen years, I went back to wearing only skirts. I gave away all of my jewelry and got rid of my makeup. I cleaned house and my closet. I removed any item that I felt was not living up to what God wanted for my life. And I haven't looked back since.

It's amazing the liberty that I now feel. In giving up my will to His, I don't feel bound. I feel more freedom than I have ever felt before. I thank God for the liberty that I now feel. Secure in knowing that I am in the will of God, I am happier than I have ever been. Others may disagree, but I know as sure as I am alive, that God has led me to this place. I am happy. I am free. I am growing in my relationship with God.

God was so patient with me to take me from here to there and back again. I feel like David when he said in Psalm 66:16: "Come and hear, all ye that fear God, and I will declare what he hath done for my soul." "I have not hid thy righteousness within my heart; I have declared thy faithfulness and thy salvation: I have not concealed thy lovingkindness and thy truth from the great congregation." (Psalm 40: 10). Hopefully, someone will be blessed by what God has done for me.

This is my testimony in a nutshell. Some who read this book will strongly disagree with what I have to say. Although some parts of this book might be controversial to both sides, I ask only that you hear me out and search the scriptures *for yourself.*

For you to fully understand my 360° turn, I have to explain what happened from the beginning. My journey from here to there and back again has left me with a better understanding of holiness standards and why they are important for the church.

This book is about my journey to that understanding.

## BACK TO THE BEGINNING

Allow me to tell my testimony, which goes back to when I was just twelve years old. I was a typical pre-teen, in love with all the frivolous things of youth: music, friends, and fun. It wasn't that I didn't think about God. It's just that other things were more prevalent in my mind, such as whether I would get new earrings for my next birthday.

I come from a good middle-class, church-going family: executive managers, community advocates, business owners, a lawyer, medical professionals, war veterans, even a couple of preachers. We were the kind of people you generally want to live next door to. On Sundays we went to church, ate big dinners, and got along well with those around us.

We went to typical denominational churches during my childhood. I attended youth programs and Sunday School, and participated in all the age appropriate activities. When I was twelve years old, I invited Jesus into my heart as my personal Savior. Water baptism was not required, and reference to the Holy Ghost was rare and almost non-existent. They certainly did not teach anything about a holiness lifestyle other than loving your neighbor and don't break any of the Ten Commandments and that sort of thing. So, it was with some surprise that God began dealing with my heart specifically about holiness.

It happened rather suddenly. One day I was a carefree almost-teenager. And another, I began feeling God's conviction when I would choose certain outfits from my wardrobe. Because I had not been taught holiness standards, I asked my grandmother about it, but she gave me vague answers and asked me not to bother her with those questions. Most likely she did not know the answers herself. Meanwhile, the conviction became stronger. I remember my grandmother getting upset at me once because I did not want to attend a wedding reception with her because my dress was sleeveless. I stood there crying and trying to make her understand that I didn't want to wear the outfit. She, not understanding what was happening with me, demanded that I stop my foolishness and wear the pretty dress. She won, as she was older and bigger. But I knew that I would need answers going forward about other things – like makeup, and my new earrings, and not wanting to wear pants anymore - so I decided to ask the pastor of the church where I was attending.

You should have seen the look on my dear pastor's face when I told him that I felt that God did not want me to wear shorts during gym. The pastor, bless his heart, was a seasoned and kind man from our evangelical church where membership and belief in Jesus Christ was all it took to make it to heaven. By all accounts the pastor was sincere, and to the best of my knowledge a good man who was just trying to do the right thing. Yet, there I stood in all my pre-teen earnestness, solemnly waiting for an answer from one who had no idea what to tell me. It would have been funny had it not been such a poignant moment.

He wasn't to blame. The church he pastored had no standards. I don't mean that they had no standards in the sense that they were all hell-raisers running around in immorality. Just the opposite. These were good church-going people who loved God and were doing the best they knew how to do. In fact, most of the ladies did not wear much make-up, only modest jewelry, and they only wore pants outside of church. The men wouldn't be caught dead in public with bare chests or pinky rings or anything like that. I just mean that they had no set standards because it apparently never occurred to them that there should be such a thing.

So, there I stood before him, asking him why I felt these convictions and could he write a letter to my gym teacher explaining that I no longer wanted to wear shorts. After a bit of thought, he agreed to look into it and get back to me. A few days later, after giving it much thought as he promised, he informed me that it was ok to wear shorts, suggested that I didn't need a note, and sent me on my way.

Except in my heart, I knew he was wrong. No one had taught me this. No one had crammed it down my throat. No one had told me that I would burn in hell if I wore makeup or jewelry or neon-bright halter tops. But somehow, I knew that God was speaking to my soul, and so at 12 years old, I embarked on a difficult crusade that would reap ridicule, confusion, and public embarrassment from family, never mind my peers. I decided to dress in skirts only anyway.

I had no support system for my decision. My family was not apostolic. They were good people. They gave at the office and in the pew. They were pillars of the community, but not of the same mind as I. Frankly, they probably thought I was losing mine.

That's not to say that apostolics were non-existent in our town. In fact, unknown to me, there was a small independent store-front church just a mile or so away from where I lived. It might as well have been a hundred miles because I didn't know they were there. There were two United Pentecostal Churches (UPC) within a ten mile radius, but I had never heard of them. And there were several independent apostolic churches within thirty miles. Any of these churches would have been glad to explain the things I didn't know, but alas I was only twelve, and understandably searching out churches I had never heard of was not on the top of my list.

So on that bright summer day, a few days from the beginning of school, I left that meeting with my pastor more confused and betwixt than before. If I wore the shorts, I would be ignoring what I felt God was saying to me. If I didn't wear the shorts, I risked a bad grade in gym and I would have to answer to my father for something that I couldn't even understand myself. Was this some strange, unique message God was sending to just me? I had no idea there were churches that taught these things so I thought I was all alone.

A few weeks after this strange conversation with my pastor, my grandmother left that church over some argument or the other with an associate minister. She began visiting other churches in search of a new church home. One day, as my grandmother and I were out in our front yard, we noticed a lady, who lived a block or two away but with whom we had not had the opportunity to be friendly, walk by our front gate. She stopped at the corner and just stood. Our curiosity peaked, so we watched covertly until a few minutes later when a church van pulled up and she got in. My grandmother, in her unique way, said "Hmm. She must be going to church." And with that she continued gardening. The next time my grandmother saw her, she asked her if she was going to church. The woman answered yes, and my grandmother asked if she could come along with her the following Sunday. The woman again answered yes, and the rest is history.

The church the lady attended was a United Pentecostal Church (UPC). We were probably the easiest souls she had ever won to the Lord. We pretty much invited ourselves. To my amazement, the church taught holiness in clothing choices and discouraged the wearing of pants for ladies. I was shocked. I had no idea that there was a church that actually taught these things.

Finding a UPC church was helpful to me in my walk with God. But I want to make it clear that my holiness standards did not come from a UPC church. God was dealing with me about gender distinction in clothing choices and about not wearing makeup or jewelry well before I landed in a UPC church. Maybe that's why I am so sure of my own standards and I am able to recognize when a church is maybe going "too far."

I sympathize with those who follow certain restrictions only out of obligation to the pastor, or family tradition, or for reasons other than a true conviction. I suppose if someone was forcing me to do something I didn't want to do I would be bitter too. But for me, I knew what God had given me even before I ever set foot in an apostolic church, so I know what I have is real.

So, when I decided many years later that I would abandon the holiness standards that God gave me, it was not a decision that I made suddenly. It seemed, at the time, that no one else was keeping to the standards (except maybe a few die hard apostolics). It just became easier to join the crowd. While I don't stand in judgment of those who have chosen a different lifestyle, I know that for me holiness standards are right. Although I have returned to those standards now, it was a long journey. I can safely say that my original conviction and my choice to return were not orchestrated by a church or tradition.

Please do not misunderstand my purpose in writing this. I

am not trying to persuade anyone to change whatever they were taught or whatever they believe simply because I said so. It's really God's job to do the changing anyway, and He does His job so well. I am also not trying to upset anyone by the changes I have made in my own life.

Some of the people I love and respect most in this world do not believe like I do. Some of them are part of the "new generation" group of apostolics who have let their hair down a little. My goal is not to discredit them or demand that everyone reach the same conclusion that I have.

But I *do* want to encourage others to search the scriptures for themselves about holiness and holiness standards. Too many of us are just going along with whatever someone has spoon-fed us, without any personal conviction. I want to encourage people to search the scriptures for themselves to see what God might (or might not) be saying on the subject.

I think that God is concerned about every aspect of our lives, including how we present ourselves to the world as ambassadors for Christ. I encourage others to not just settle for what is comfortable, convenient, or easy. This shouldn't be an "ask-the-pastor-and-get-a-few-scriptures-then-go-on-your-merry-way" kind of search. That's just riding on the coattails of whatever someone else has been convicted of or doing what your current hang-out crowd is doing. Your search should be one that takes you into the Word, into prayer, and into consecration with God. Expect opposition if your thoughts are not popular with whatever crowd you are with. That's ok. In the end, because you sought the will of God, you will know for sure what He wants for your life. If you sincerely want to understand holiness, I challenge you to commit yourself to prayer and searching the scriptures. I believe God will lead you and guide you into truth because that's the kind of caring God He is.

Secondly, I am sharing my story because I want to give God glory for what He has done for me, plain and simple. This is my testimony. Someone else's testimony might be different. But as for me, I want to give God praise for this incredible journey.

## WHO INVENTED HOLINESS ANYWAY?

What exactly is a holiness lifestyle? To be holy is to be dedicated or consecrated for the purposes of God. Anything that is unholy is unclean; an abomination to God is unclean; ungodly things are unclean; things that reflect the world values and customs more than God's are unclean. Merriam-Webster says that a lifestyle is a typical way of life or an indication of the interests, beliefs, or behavior orientations of a particular person or group. The Business Dictionary defines lifestyle as a way of living which is made visually clear by the way in which one conducts herself on a daily basis. The dictionary further says that a lifestyle reflects a person's self-image or self-concept. Therefore, it can be said that a holiness lifestyle refers to the typical behaviors of a person, who is striving to remain consecrated and dedicated to God, and which is a reflection of the person's self-concept.

Those who engage in a holiness lifestyle often apply this lifestyle to their clothing choices. The concept is that holiness should apply both on the inside and on the outside. In I Corinthians 6:20, Paul told the church to glorify God in their body (flesh). Most of us understand glorifying God by our words (verbal praise). Glorifying God by our actions (service to him) is not an uncommon concept. But I Corinthians 6:20 tells us that we must *also* glorify God in how we present our bodies.

God's interest in how we treat our bodies, and how we clothe our bodies, is nothing new. From the beginning – even when there were 'bigger" issues on the forefront like the heavy weight of sin that had just fallen on mankind by Adam and Eve eating the fruit – God took the time to stop and provide clothing that He saw fit for Adam and Eve. He could have told them to work it out on their own because it made no difference to Him. There was no hurry since they were husband and wife and the only two people on the planet at the time – not really a big deal if they saw each other naked. But even in the beginning, clothing was important enough to God to stop and do it right.

God told the Hebrews in Leviticus 11:44 to be holy because He is holy. The people of God understood this. They knew that in order to be consecrated and separated for God, they were going to do things differently than the mainstream societies that were all around them. In I Chronicles 16:29, when David was offering up praise to God for his goodness (verse 7 – 36), his equated holiness with worship and referred to holiness as beautiful.

From the beginning, when God selected His chosen people, he decided they would be a holy people.[1] The children of Israel were admonished to practice holiness regarding their bodies. For example, God instructed Israel in Leviticus 19:28 to not print on their bodies (today we call it tattooing). Although God did not demand head covering for women in the Old Testament – that was a cultural requirement that reflected society's view of women - He did tell His people not to cross-dress in Deuteronomy 22:5. In Exodus chapter 28, God instructed Moses to make *holy* garments for Aaron.

---

[1] Ephesians 1:4 (KJV)

Later on in the New Testament, the apostle Paul reminded the Corinthian church that their bodies were the temple of God[2]. Everyone knows that temples are to be holy because they are a reflection of the God that is worshipped on the inside. Paul took it a step further and equated the Christian body to a temple. Just as a physical temple is deemed holy, so is the Christian body. Paul, in making this analogy, was telling the Corinthian church that their bodies were to be consecrated to God.

I believe that God wants me to dress modestly and in a holy manner. My entire lifestyle should be a reflection of my relationship with God, and a testimony of what He has done in my life. I also believe that holiness standards should apply to both male and female. People get caught up with the "pants" issue and so some people don't think that men have any dress standards. I disagree. Christian men should also wear outfits that reflect modesty and holiness. Yes, there is a gender distinction with women wearing skirts and dresses, and men wearing pants. But there is more to it than that. We still have the scriptural

---

[2] I Corinthians 3:16 (KJV)

requirement of holiness and the scriptural requirement of moderation. So, tight clothing – male or female – for example, is probably not a reflection of holiness. The same goes for clothing that is very thin and revealing. Clothing with writing should support godly values when worn by a Christian. Length of clothing should be considered for both male and female. Clothing that is low, sagging, or revealing when a person bends over is not godly in my opinion. These things apply whether it's a male or a female. It's not about shame or not loving your body. It's about modesty and covering your body in a holy manner.

I believe that holiness is a way of life that should reflect our Lord and Master Jesus Christ. Holiness cannot be true holiness unless it is on the inside and the outside. How many of us would accept a glass at a restaurant that is clean on the inside but with traces of food or lip print from the previous customer on the outside or vice versa? Imagine calling the waitress over, only to have her tell you that it's ok because the glass is clean on the inside. Clean is only clean if it is both clean inside and out. Our lives should reflect holiness on the inside *and* on the outside.

## 21ST CENTURY RELEVANCE: HOLINESS IS *STILL* RIGHT TODAY!

The holiness movement is not a new thing as far as modern society is concerned. It's as old as Azusa Street and speaking in tongues. If there has been any change, it has been in recent years with the church's desire to assimilate and blend with the rest of the world. Many churches are struggling today with the changing cultural climate of our world. The pressure to conform in order to fill the church pews is a real concern for many. It is difficult enough for those who were raised in this to ignore the fact that "everybody else" has given in, never mind the new and unacclimated.

Possibly the most controversial issue has been whether or not women should wear pants. It is no secret that post World War II groups began to respond to cultural changes and began to reject many of the modest dressing customs that were typical of evangelical churches of the time.

> "The relationship between pants and active women would continue throughout the 20th century: when women went to work during World War II, it was often in trousers, particularly if their jobs didn't involve working with members of the public. Though there was a constricting girdle-resurgence in the 1950s, the 1960s saw a casual-wear liberation happen just as feminism started to hit America's mainstream. Jeans exploded in popularity, symbolizing rebellion and solidarity with the working man. . . . In the 1970s and 1980s, when women were entering the workforce in earnest in America, some almost felt like pants were forced on them as part of a work uniform meant to show their parity with male colleagues. (Hence the emphasis on masculinized, shoulder-pad-heavy styles.) Pat Schroeder, the first woman elected to Congress from Colorado, recalls showing up for a photo with the handful of women then serving in that body and being criticized for wearing a dress."[3]

Such was the pressure continuing into the latter part of the 20th century. As more and more religious groups "changed" their stance on the issue of pants, others followed suit. "Today, pants are worn far more often than skirts by women, and many women wear pants almost all the time."[4] Along with the pants issue,

---

[3]Steinmetz, Katy. "From Horse People to Hillary Clinton: A History of Women Wearing Pants" Women and History. *Time,* 2006, June 14. Accessed 2017, April 27.
[4] Holea, G. "Women and Pants" History and Women. *Patzer, Mirella S*, 2012, April 12. Accessed 2017, April 27.

more and more groups began to relax their standards on jewelry and cosmetics. It became rare to find a church that actively preached against those things.

By the start of the 21st century, those who held to the traditional standards were in the minority, even among apostolic groups. Eventually, some groups began to disparage those who kept to holiness standards and accuse them of legalism. While we accept dresses for certain groups on the fringes of society, such as the Amish or strict Mennonites, most church groups accept pants wearing as a given for even women in the pulpit. Consequently, the concept of holiness standards is foreign to many in the church world, even among those who profess devout Christianity. Many churches do not even mention the word, and even fewer still advocate for it. Love, peace, and joy are much safer subjects. One could listen to any number of Christian radio stations for hours and not hear a single song croon about the attributes of holiness. It's just not popular.

One would tend to wonder about the lack of mention of his attribute so important that the Bible says no one will see God without it.[5] Could it be that church folks of today see holiness as an impossible standard, such that we actually expect to see people living a lifestyle of unholiness? Or, is it that we believe holiness to be an archaic and irrelevant concept, relegated to those living in the 50's and decades gone by?

Holiness is definitely not pop-culture cute. Many young adults do not consider the concepts of holiness, including dress standards, as hip enough for the 21st century. It's not considered sophisticated enough for the suave, educated, and elite. It's not satisfying enough for the culturally enlightened.

The concept of living a different lifestyle is very strange to many. Some adults have never heard their church speak against abstinence, alcohol, cigarettes, and certainly not immodest dress. Many don't know for sure what things are considered unholy anymore since "everybody" is doing it. Sometimes the only time a person hears a preacher mention holiness/unholiness is in a brief humorous story about carousing or some other extreme behavior in order to make a point in a

---

[5] Hebrews 12:14 (KJV)

sermon. Such mention generally creates a chuckle within the congregation. I note that a well-known playwright, whose target audience is supposedly church folks, repeatedly finds humor in the immoral lifestyle and "behind closed doors" shenanigans of churchgoers. One minute the characters are involved in all kinds of behavior one would expect to see on a soap opera, and the next the characters break out into praise and worship. And somehow this is extremely funny – and acceptable - to the audience. It's no wonder that the lines have blurred for many people. Sad to say, the church is possibly more confused than the world.

Some say that holiness is only an "inside" issue. They say that as long as your heart is clean on the inside, then what you wear on the outside is unimportant. My search of the scriptures does not lead me to the same conclusion. I find that the Bible has many scriptures where God says holiness applies to the outside also. It is also a strange analysis since we expect other aspects of Christianity that begin on the inside to "spill over" or show up on the outside. Worship, joy, peace, and sharing what God has done *in* your heart are all things that originate on the inside. Yet, we generally expect those things to spill over to the outside. What's the difference with holiness?

Another deflection to the subject is the claim that there are other considerations to holiness living besides dress standards. Well, that's true and fairly obvious. There is more to living for God than just a hemline. Furthermore, holiness is only one part of pleasing God, but not the totality of pleasing God. Dress standards do not save us, period. None of us are ready for heaven without being born again, regardless of whether we wear our sleeves to the fingertips or not. But after being born again, it is imperative that a Christian lives a clean lifestyle. And that lifestyle must include both what's on the inside as well as the outside.

Some people question the logic of holiness. If God loves me just the way I am, even as a dirty, filthy sinner, why does it matter anyway? If God loves me when I was sinning, He will surely love me when I am a "Christian" even if my dress standard is not what it should be. This train of thought might lead one to question any boundary that God has placed in his life. Because if

God loves me no matter what I do, then by extension it doesn't matter what I do. If I don't have to follow any rules then it doesn't matter. And if, God isn't making me do what I don't want to do, then nobody else can tell me what to do either. It's a slippery slope.

It is a faulty argument because, first of all, God calls us into change, not to remain the same. Change is what coming to God is all about. II Corinthians 2:15 says that when a person comes into a new relationship with Christ, he is a new creature. Old things are passed away. *All* things become new. Your heart becomes new. Your way of thinking becomes new. Your lifestyle becomes new.

And almost hand in hand with newness comes separation. Time and time again, the scriptures tell us that God wants us to separate ourselves from the things of the world. The world's concepts are not God's. That's the old stuff. We used to think a certain way. We used to live our lives a certain way. When God comes in, He makes it *all* new. New heart. New mindset. New lifestyle.

Second, it's meshing the issues. God loves us just the way we come into the world, and we each came into the world with sin. Just because God loves us unconditionally, it does not mean that He loves *the way we are.* Even though He loves us from the beginning before we were even born, I Timothy 2:4 says that He still wants each of us to be saved. God loves each of us unconditionally, but He isn't always pleased with the lifestyle we each choose.

Third, love is not a synonym for blindness. The fact remains that some people will not make it to heaven because of their own free choices. The scriptures clearly tell us this. Yet God loves those people just the same as He loves the one sitting on the church pew. And if God can love the person that is not going to make it to heaven, then that means that there will be people in hell that God loves. It's His love that caused Him to die on the cross. But it's our choice where we want to spend eternity. His love does not mean he will overlook our choices. So, we can't negate or ignore the issue of holiness just because God loves us unconditionally.

Holiness is not a bad word. I Corinthians 5:16 – 17, tells us to be separate because we are the temple of God. This issue was so important, that when Paul sent a second letter to the Corinthian church, he brought it up again, urging them to reach for holiness, and to cleanse their flesh (the outside) as well as the spirit (the inside.)[6] In Romans 12:1, the church was adamantly told to present their bodies as a holy sacrifice. I Thessalonians 3:13 tells us to *establish* our hearts in holiness. Ephesians 5:27 tells us that Christ wants a holy church.

Why did the scriptures continuously remind the early church to remain separate and holy? The answer is found in I Peter 2:9, where they are told that they were chosen, holy, and peculiar (different) so that they could give God praise. Yes, God wants holy people so that our lifestyle would be praise to Him!

Given that many apostolic churches today are choosing to relax their standards, even fellow believers might tread on your beliefs because your choices make them feel uncomfortable, and they don't get where you are coming from. This can rattle a

---

[6] II Corinthians 7:1 (KJV)

believer who is already being tempted to forgo his or her convictions.

Holiness is fitting for any person who professes to be a servant of God. Psalms 93: 5 says that holiness becomes God's house, not just for the moment, but forever! Google defines "becomes" as "to look good on or suit (someone)." In other words, holiness will always look good on God's people.

Church folks fervently disagree on what *specific* things are unholy, and how the scriptures apply to the modern world. However, what is not disputable is that God does require holiness, and it is applicable to the New Testament church. Hebrews 12:14 says that without holiness *no man* shall see the Lord. In other words, there is no going to heaven or seeing Jesus face to face without holiness. All the money in the world or fancy programs or famous names will not give us a free pass into heaven – we have to have holiness.

So, is holiness in the way we dress still an appropriate instruction for the 21st century church? Based on the scriptures, the answer is a resounding, yes! We can't compartmentalize our walk with God, i.e. "I'll serve God in my heart, but not in my lifestyle" or "I'll represent God in my verbal testimony, but not in how I present myself in public." There are no scriptures – that I found anyway – that support that divided concept. Holiness is still right for the 21st century church, and holiness is relevant for all aspects of a Christian's life.

## THE DEBATE:
## THE ARGUMENT FOR HOLINESS

The way a person dresses is a portrayal of their values and their personality. It is what many people use to either fit in or to stand out from a crowd. Even the media, which many of us bend over backwards to imitate, agree that fashion is a reflection of who one is. Psychologist and Professor Karen Pine, in her article (and her book), "Mind What You Wear," discussed both how you choose your clothes, and, shockingly, how your clothes choose you.[7] She did quite a bit of research on the effect of fashion on lifestyles and vice versa. Dr. Pine states in her book that clothes actually have the power to change the way of thinking of the wearer. She says that just a simple tweak can literally be life-changing. I am not suggesting that Dr. Pine is a companion in my beliefs, but her research validates the concept that clothing has a significant impact on image and lifestyle. We have long

---

[7]Pine, Karen Dr. "Mind What You Wear: It Can Change Your Life" Huffington Post. *Huffington Post,* 2014, May 21. Accessed 2017. April 27.

suspected that what a person is already feeling can be manifested by what he or she wears. Other studies have shown that women who wear longer skirts in the workplace come across as more competent.[8] My point is that even the world agrees to some extent that what you wear makes a difference on how you are perceived.

We have already established that holiness is about more than just dressing. A holiness lifestyle is more than just where your hemline falls or whether you wear shorts or not to play basketball. God requires a contrite heart and a pure heart. We are to reflect his grace and holiness in all that we do, say or think. Holiness is an inside *and* an outside job. A holiness lifestyle is a reflection of our human obedience to God so that we can be what He wants us to be both inside and out.

Moving on from that point, it is important to emphasize what holiness is not. It is *not* about perfection. If that was the case, none of us would qualify and none of us would make it to heaven. Holiness is also *not* an instantaneous thing; it is a

---

[8] Fletcher, Ben Dr. "What Your Clothes Might Be Saying About You" Psychology Today. *Psychology Today,* 2013, April 20. Accessed 2017., April 27.

continual process of living dedicated to God.

Some people see holiness as a bunch of arbitrary rules by a preacher to limit their freedom and joy in life. That's *not* what holiness is about. Holiness is a chosen lifestyle that is a result of God renewing a mind. Forced decisions will not result in inner change. Holiness is *not* about a bunch of arbitrary rules. It is a choice to conduct our lives in a way that is representative of God and pleasing to Him.

True, holiness does require boundaries. We have freedom in God, but it is important that we live the way He wants us to live. The Bible provides us with a plethora of guidelines for Christian living. For example, the scriptures tell us to "abstain," or restrain, from the appearance of evil.[9] I Corinthians 6:18 tells us to "flee," or run away as though in danger, from fornication. Romans 6:12 - 13 tells us to keep sin from having authority in our own bodies, and to not "yield" to tools of unrighteousness. Galatians 5:19 – 21 gives a long list of things not to do if you want to make it into the kingdom of God (hint: it's more than the

---

[9] I Thessalonians 5:22 (KJV)

10 commandments). Furthermore, Romans 13:1 tells us to be obedient to those in authority; I Corinthians 6:1 – 4 tells us that we are not permitted to take our brethren to court; Proverbs 3:27 – 28 tells us to bless our neighbor when we have the ability to do so; I Corinthians 10:10 tells us to quit complaining; II Corinthians 9:7 says to be a cheerful giver, and so forth. My point is that boundaries and rules are a natural part of the equation.

This is no different than any other aspect of life. We dress a certain way – and avoid certain outfits - to a wedding or a job interview or to appear in court or to meet future in-laws. We understand that certain situations should require a certain amount of decorum or we strive to "represent" by the way we present ourselves. In any other aspect of life, most of us understand rules and boundaries, both physical and symbolic. We allow someone else to tell us when to show up for work, and when to leave. We follow customs and patterns about even the most private areas of our lives – we eat eggs in the morning and mashed potatoes at night. We keep our children from not walking in the street or tell them to not play in a certain yard, not because we want to curb their fun, but because we establish boundaries to protect them. We exit through certain doors and enter through others, often without thought or reason, because someone else tells us to do it this way or that. Really, it doesn't matter what side of the debate you are on, my point is that boundaries are an important and necessary part of life. Generally, it's not a conversation we shy away from – unless of course it relates to dress standards.

I think this is just a trick of the enemy. The enemy has always tried to get us to buck against God's rules and His ways of protecting us. From the beginning, he has tried to make us believe that God's ways are extreme and unnecessary and too rigid. Remember, the enemy's first conversation with Eve? The first thing he did was to question the boundaries that God had placed there for her. At the time, the boundary did not make sense to Eve, as it might not have for me either if I was in her position. I would probably have argued that it made no difference what I ate. After all, God is about love and peace and joy. Let's be honest, that's what most of us would have thought.

Something as simple as a biodegradable fruit???!!! Come on! How could what I eat affect my relationship with God? How could a tiny simple fruit or piece of jewelry, or a piece of clothing affect my eternity with God? The enemy has done this many times in the scriptures, and if I be honest, in my life. He confuses the issue by having us focus on the unimportant elements. He makes it seem as though we are being deprived by walking within the boundaries that God has placed in our lives. And it works today just like it worked on Eve in the garden.

Eve had also forgotten that obedience is a type of worship. No one had more boundaries and do-this-don't-do-that rules than the children of Israel. But it really wasn't about the rules. It's not that God was merely interested in the blind following of rituals and sacrifices. Obedience to God's commandments and following holiness was also a type of worship to God. Sacrifice is only acceptable when it is offered in worship.

Boundaries are not there to curb our fun. The guidelines in the Bible are there for our protection. Even when we don't understand God's purpose, we can be sure that He loves us and if God says it, then it must be right. Boundaries are a natural part of any relationship equation because not everything that looks good is best. When God lays boundaries, and communicates that by His Word and by spiritual leaders that He has established in a Christian's life, that's not legalism. That's just a heavenly Father that sees the big picture a little better than us, and wants us to trust Him and serve him with our obedience.

## IT'S PERSONAL

Holiness living is a continuous process. As Jesus told the disciples, He will lead and guide into all truth. He said this to the disciples even at a point when they were already called and chosen to be on God's team. But God still had to disciple them and show them how to live. Likewise, just being born-again is not the end of the journey. It's just the beginning. And so, holiness is something that should be practiced each day. It's part of the journey in living for God.

This Christian journey with God is a personal journey. But, that doesn't mean that each person makes up his own personal rules as he goes along. There aren't ten roads to heaven – there is only one way and the roadmap is in the scriptures. John chapter 3 lets us know that God already has *one* plan on how we will get to heaven, not several based on whatever one's imagination might come up with. But it does mean that each person's pace – whether fast, moderate, or slow as molasses - is unique to that individual. As our heavenly Father, God knows where we each stand and will reveal things to the individual at different points so long as that individual remains contrite before him. Most parents will be able to relate to this analogy: A father will most likely teach all of his children the same values, but he might not teach a lesson at exactly the same point in each child's life. That's because each child is unique. Some catch on to certain concepts sooner than others. Personality comes into play. Some children are more compliant than others. The method of teaching might be different because one child might be a visual learner, another might be a verbal learner. Some children will hear their parent give a particular instruction and immediately obey. Still another child might learn only after there is a consequence or something goes awry. For another child it might take several mishaps, and bumps and bruises, before she gets the concept. The same is true in our walk with God. God as our heavenly Father introduces things into our lives at different stages because He knows us better than anyone else and knows when we are ready to receive. Each person's spiritual growth spurts are unique, but if you stay focused on God, instead of a religious group, then God will certainly lead you.

For example, some people adapt a standard of dress because it is what their pastor believes. In essence they are blindly following a church without any real convictions of their own. Their standard is based on their respect for their pastor or church. But the same can be said for the other end of the spectrum. Some people allow the lack of standards to influence their choices of dress. They reject holiness dress standards because they attend a church that says that holiness standards are not required. And without searching the scriptures or seeking God in prayer and fasting, they simply dismiss the issue because it is more convenient to accept what they are being taught (or not being taught).

It is important for Christians to be aware that each person has to work out their own salvation[10]. Forcing someone one way or the other is not helpful or productive. I don't know about you,

---

[10] Philippians 2:12 (KJV)

but I can't change anyone's heart anyway, so why even try. The result is just going to be messy and confusing. And getting someone to dress a certain way without a change of heart is not going to produce a sanctified soul; it will be just window dressing for a heart that is not convinced. We don't have a heaven or hell to put anyone in, but God surely does, so it is important for us to let Him do the work while we stand back. It's an individual decision.

So, I ask a fundamental question just as the crowd asked the disciples in Acts chapter 2: what shall we do? What is it going to take to make a change to a holiness lifestyle if I am not already living it? The answer is *a change of mind.* It is no wonder that to the same church that God instructed to separate themselves, He also told them to renew or change their mind. That is because holiness is not just about a bunch of rules: do this, don't do that. Holiness is the lifestyle that results when you allow God to *change your mind.* In telling the church to present their bodies – not just their hearts – as a holy sacrifice, Romans 12:1 – 2 tells the church to transform themselves by renewing their minds. Google defines “transform” as to “make a thorough and dramatic change.” Merriam-Webster defines “renewing” as the process of making like new; restoration to freshness, vigor, or perfection. In other words, in order to achieve this standard of holiness, in order to achieve this transformation, or a thorough and dramatic change, one has to go through a process of making his mind like new. Simply stated, it takes a *change of mind.*

## LEGALISM

It is impossible to fully talk about holiness without addressing the issue of legalism. The term "legalism" has been used often to describe a church's view on holiness standards. Those who say that it is legalism to establish doctrinal guidelines also say that a church or a pastor has no right to tell another Christian what they should or should not wear. Each person must decide what works for himself, they say. They deem the church or doctrine as spewing forth rules that are not biblical. Clothing and dress standards are not an important part of the Christian walk, they contend, and anyone who tries to suggest otherwise is into control and bondage. Often the word is thrown into a conversation without warning, like how the word "fanatic" was used in the 80's to tone down Christians who were too passionate about their conversion.

Now the new attack word for Christianity is legalism.

Legalism refers to a set of man-made rules or a belief that certain "works" guarantees a person's entry through the pearly gates. Such thinking, of course, would be faulty because we are saved by grace.

Grace is God giving us what we do not deserve. Salvation is by grace – we do not deserve salvation, and there is nothing that we could possibly do to earn it. If we worked forever, and did all that was in our power to do, we would still not earn enough brownie points for grace. If we labored all our lives, and then at the end of our life, approached God for our deserved paycheck for all the goodness in our life, it would still be death. But God, in His *grace*, decided to offer a free gift of salvation. It's not anything we worked for, it's simply His gift. That's grace. "For the wages of sin is death; but the gift of God is eternal life through Jesus Christ our Lord." [11]

But just as flawed is the opposite concept that declares a mere belief in Jesus Christ is *all* that a Christian needs to do in order to *remain* saved. If that was the case, then the devil is also

---

[11]Romans 6:12 (KJV)

on his way to heaven, because the Bible says that he believes so much that he trembles.[12] So, evidently, it takes more than belief.

Let's say, for instance, that you decide to go to a friend's home - an appropriate example, I think, because entry into heaven is entry into God's home. Say, for example, your friend, Suzie, invites you to a very special and fancy dinner party at her home, and black tie is required. Three things need to happen in order to *gain entry* to the dinner party: Number one, you have to accept the invitation. Second, because it's her invitation, she gets to choose the criteria for attendance. So, you will have to don your tuxedo or formal outfit if you want to get in. Third, you have to actually show up. Telling her that you believe she is having a dinner party and that you think it's great will not automatically transport you into her home. You have to actually get dressed, and get into your car and drive to your friend's home. You have to *do* something. While we are saved by grace, God still expects us to *do* what he has asked us to do. James told the early church, "Even so faith, if it hath not works, is dead,

[12] James 2:19 (KJV)

being alone. Yea, a man may say, Thou hast faith, and I have works: shew me thy faith without thy works, and I will shew thee my faith by my works."[13]

Ok, so now you are at the dinner party in Suzie's home. What now? Just because you gained entrance, would you be allowed to stay regardless of any subsequent misbehavior? Probably not. First of all, if you show up in cut-off shorts and a dirty t-shirt, or no shirt at all, your friend will likely pull you aside and ask you politely to leave. If you show up in the correct attire, and gain entrance, chances are you will not be allowed to walk all over her white sofa, make fun of her other guests, rifle through her closets, or throw her dog off the patio. In other words, she will have rules of conduct, and if you don't follow those rules, then you will probably be reprimanded.

Dress standards and behavior guidelines are also common in other areas of our modern society, and generally, people do not complain as much as they do with church standards. Many social and civic groups, such as youth organizations, have dress codes.

---

[13] James 2: 17 – 18 (KJV)

They demand that all members adhere to these rules, and generally, there is no "real" benefit, or even logic, to the requirement, other than "it's tradition." Employers of office workers impose dress codes based on a higher up's perception of what is "acceptable." There is no proof that a person's filing productivity increases more in business wear. In fact, because it is more comfortable, they might actually work faster in denim. But employers demand, and we comply, usually without much complaining. Yet, somehow it becomes difficult for Christians to accept that God might also have a preference about what we wear and how we present ourselves.

I shake my head when I hear the misapplication of the term "legalism" to holiness standards. Legalism, by definition, is ignoring the biblical truth that salvation is freely given *through* God and His grace, and declaring that salvation is earned by a person's human actions. But usually, people misuse it to refer to a church or doctrine that the speaker finds arbitrarily controlling. They declare that standards cannot be biblical because we are saved by grace. The slippery slope on this thinking is steep because if a church is condemned for denouncing one lifestyle or dress standard that they find biblically offensive, then they certainly don't have the authority to reprimand *any* lifestyle or dress standard.

With the high cry of legalism so common now among churches, some leaders are afraid to speak out against anything that might be unpopular. While this is not a problem everywhere, it is a slippery slope because once you remove the landmarks, it leaves the door open for anything and everything.

I am not saying that legalism does not exist. It is true that some churches have imposed their own rules where there is no biblical basis. In some cases, a church might have allowed their fears or tradition to dictate certain lifestyles. I acknowledge this because although I have been blessed to have good pastors in my life, I hear this complaint enough to realize that there must be some truth to it.

I sympathize with anyone who finds themselves in this position. Certainly it is a person's right to choose. God does not force us to do anything, and neither should mere humans. There are consequences to disobedience that only God will mete out in the end. After all, we don't have a heaven or hell to put anyone in. Forced compliance is not real compliance, and without a real change of mind it's not going to last anyway.

But I understand the need for boundaries. It is sometimes said that there is a paternal nature to pastoring. I'm not a pastor, and I don't pretend to know all that the job entails. But, I think I understand enough to know that pastors are looking out for the souls of those they lead. It's a tough job to pastor a group of people even on the best of days. Nonetheless, each person has the right to make up his own mind, and should be able to do so without fear of condemnation or reprisal. Although holiness is scripturally based, Hosea 6:6 says, "For I desired mercy, and not sacrifice; and the knowledge of God more than burnt offerings."

Yet, even for those extreme cases, I have never heard of any church that would ask someone to leave because of the way the person is dressed. And I have been to a lot of apostolic churches, because my career, and other reasons, has afforded me the opportunity to travel a little. I have been to apostolic services across the east and west, north and south, and a few in-between and a few overseas: New York, New Jersey, California, Texas, Oklahoma, West Virginia, Pennsylvania, North Carolina, South Carolina, Georgia, Florida, Alabama, Tennessee, Kentucky, Ohio, Michigan, Indiana, Illinois, Wisconsin – I'm sure you get the picture. Not once in any of those churches have I ever seen anyone escorted from the premises, or disrespected, or told not to participate in worship because of what they were wearing.

But it is appropriate for a church, as an organization representing God and their beliefs, to have guidelines for their leadership, just the same as your friend Suzie might have rules and guidelines about behavior in her home. That's not legalism. They are not saying that a long skirt or sleeve length is going to get you into heaven. That would be ludicrous. But, it is important to understand that God has a certain way He wants us to behave once we have joined *His* kingdom. Being born again means change, in one word. That's a change to the inside, a change to your lifestyle - including how you dress, how you carry yourself, how you think about yourself – and a change to behavior.

Because people are not willing to put boundaries on their dress standards, I have seen embarrassing examples of inappropriate clothes being worn by those in church leadership and those on the platform: teachers with revealing cleavages; members in clothing that were extremely too tight or revealing (I'm talking about both genders); costumes that brought more attention to the outfit itself than the person inside the outfit, and so on. I say embarrassing because it is disconcerting considering who we profess to be.

Holiness is not about legalism. They are not even related. Holiness is about worship to God and presenting your body as a living sacrifice to him in a way that is pleasing to God. Just like in other areas of life, it is necessary to have boundaries. Spiritual boundaries are not about control so long as it is supported by scripture. Spiritual boundaries are about following the principles that God wants in the lives of His children.

## KEEPING IT REAL FOR THE LADIES

So, we have established that holiness is still relevant for the church today. Holiness is important in all aspects of a Christian's life. God wants us to be holy because He is a holy God. We have established that how we dress and present ourselves is not the total picture. It's not all about a hemline or how far your sleeves come down your arm. But those things are important in the proper context.

But I have to put a word in for the ladies. Men have no idea how challenging it can become. This might be a bit uncomfortable to hear, so keep reading only if you dare.

Honestly speaking, shopping is more of a hunt for women who wear only dresses and skirts. For one thing, it can be quite a quest to find quality products that fit the holiness lifestyle, especially if you are *not* a size 6 (hint: I'm talking about me). And, it is twice as hard if you are looking for professional clothing while trying to keep your hemline right.

Just keeping it real, it can also be pricey to live a separated lifestyle. I have been there and done that. I went from an almost all pants wardrobe to an all skirts/dresses wardrobe, and it was painful, even for someone like me who enjoys a good shopping trip. Adding the cost of slips and things like that, it is much cheaper to dress like the mainstream. (It's no wonder apostolic women shop all the time!) For me, trying to undo what had already been done was tough. The salespeople were probably high-fiving each other as they saw me coming.

Finding dresses was not the problem. But, finding a *conservative* dress was. In case you haven't noticed, dresses are making a come-back. More dresses are on the racks now than there has been in recent years. Everything from maxis to minis, dressy to casual. The fashion runway has embraced the feminine. But that fact hasn't made the process easier. That's because fashion designers aren't creating with apostolics in mind: spaghetti straps, no sleeves, and splits up the wazoo.

Dresses may be the new norm, but do they all have to be

sleeveless? I am tired of finding a cute little number in the perfect color only to realize that it won't work. It's as though the fashion designers think that if they give in to dresses then there must be some concession with the sleeve, the hemline, or the neckline. By the way, what's with the "cap sleeves" which is almost no sleeve at all, just a small scrap of fabric sticking out from the shoulder masquerading as real sleeves?

If you are a professional woman or work outside of the home in any capacity, there is an additional challenge. In some professions, like an office environment or teaching, women wear both slacks and skirts. So it's easier to get by. In other professions, like increasingly in the medical field, women wear slacks all the time. Long gone are the days when nurses wore those cute white dresses. Today, most medical professionals are wearing scrubs. So some professions create additional challenges that are unfamiliar to the rest of us.

I'm speaking out about the inconvenience and reality of a modest dress choice because I think it is a real issue for women. It is an honest discussion because men have no idea what we go through. It's not merely an excuse. It's not empty grumbling just for the sake of complaining. It's real talk – unique to women perhaps, but just as real. It really is a challenge when we go to the stores, and when we venture into the workplace, especially so if you live in an area with limited shopping options.

This brings me to another (painful) point that only women can relate to in this dress-pants issue. Some women, especially new converts, are deterred from this lifestyle because the examples they see around them are women who are wearing boring and unfashionable clothing. If we are not careful, we can easily give the incorrect impression that they will have to look positively drab in order to serve God. And it's scary for them because the world gives the impression that a woman cannot be attractive in her own right without applying makeup and jewelry. When we give the wrong impression, they are afraid that they will have to look positively drab in order to serve God.

The truth is that no woman wants to appear in public looking unattractive. Most of us want to do the best we can with what God has given us. So it's disconcerting when we see church members looking like they just stepped off the pages of the latest Pioneers Fashion magazine. Can you imagine how that comes across to someone new to the faith? They are trying their best not to run with all the speed they can muster in their fashionable feet.

I think repentance is in order, myself included. We do God a disservice when we dress homely and unattractive. Whether we realize it or not, our appearance is what people see before we even open our mouth to share a scripture. Our appearance can be a deterrent or an encouragement. It can scare people away if they think they have to look homely and unattractive to be saved. Sometimes unbelievers or new converts look at us and walk away because we have represented Christ as dull, boring, and socially irrelevant. Holiness is very relevant to the identity of Christians in the 21st century, but sometimes I think we confuse holiness with homeliness. I think we owe God and the church a better representation than that. Can I get an "amen?"

I'm not saying we have to go to the grocery store in

uptown fashions. I certainly don't have that kind of money or closet space. But just like the person who incorrectly thinks that the *only* thing that matters is the way she dresses, it is just as incorrect to think that *how* she dresses in her skirt is unimportant.

Raise your hand if you have ever seen someone in Walmart with no smile, a shabby skirt and sneakers, looking like she just stepped out of a time capsule from 1955. I'm putting myself there too because I think I have done that a few times myself. Too hurried and busy to care what I look like while I dash into the nearest supercenter on a busy day, totally unaware of how I might appear to others. I admit that I have been guilty of doing the same. And I admit that such a presentation is not the best way to represent Christ.

I think that when we present ourselves in this old-fashioned dreary way we are giving God bad P.R. It's really - if you think about it - an un-witness to Christ. I believe that God expects us to represent Him well in the way we dress – not just our hemlines, but also our general appearance. Ecclesiastes 9:8 says "Let thy garments be always white; and thy head lack no ointment." In other words, the Bible wants us to groom ourselves and look good. Even in the case of fasting, which is a deeply spiritual experience, with no carnal merits, God tells us, "But thou, when thou fastest, anoint thine head, and wash thy face."[14]

That said, I wouldn't change a thing about my choice of dress. I have been there and done that with the challenges. Being a professional woman, I also relate to the special challenges that presents. Yet, I am very much at peace with the choices that I have made.

I have been approached by others who are curious about my choices. Ironically, I have learned that people's questions are not always because they oppose. I have learned to pause and listen to the voice of God when I get a question about how I dress. Sometimes the person really doesn't understand, and it presents an opportunity to tell them about the cross and Calvary, and how it has changed my life. Oddly enough, unbelievers sometime understand the concept of dressing holy better than those who claim affiliation with Christ. Isn't that strange?

---

[14] Matthew 6:17 (KJV)

## LESSONS FROM THE JOURNEY

So much is said about holiness standards and legalism that it is assumed by the general church world that any restriction or boundary taught by a church is oppressive and forced on the congregation. Any indication that it is the member's free choice falls on deaf ears because to them it is unimaginable that anyone would choose to follow holiness unless it was forced. Often, a person who claims to freely follow these guidelines is portrayed as brainwashed. Even some who are schooled in scriptures downplay the scriptural significance of dressing with gender distinction and dressing modestly. It is difficult for some to understand that holiness can be a freely chosen and preferred lifestyle.

I can't speak for anyone else, but I can safely say that the convictions that I have are definitely from God and not any imposed by a preacher. Before I even stepped foot into an apostolic church, God began dealing with my heart and showed me that it was important to Him how I dressed and how I presented myself as a Christian. Because I had this encounter with God early on, I understood the basis for holiness standards. While the challenges were no easier for me than they were for the next person, I knew that God wanted me to dress with gender distinction and in a modest manner that reflected my relationship with him.

Although I eventually walked away from holiness standards, I did it out of convenience and because "everyone" else was doing it. So, I get that viewpoint, too. The pressure to be like everyone else influenced me although I was never really comfortable with it. There was no pressure from my church because the church I attended did not have holiness standards for dressing. It didn't matter to them whether I did or not, so it was easy to push conviction to the back burner. During this period of my life, I learned that although I saw myself as a strong Christian, I was not immune to pressures from the world.

I learned something about fellow Christians, also. To my

surprise, I encountered many others that walked away from holiness standards and church because the conviction was never really theirs. And when the world began pressing against them, and their own minds began doubting – just like I did – they walked away with the accusation of legalism on their lips.

Grandma's religion or pastor's rules will *not* cut it when you are facing indecision or when the world is pressuring you for answers about "why" you do the things that you do. It doesn't matter how long you have been in church or the depth of your religious "pedigree." A tenth generation apostolic could fall prey just the same as someone who is new to the message. It is crucial that we determine for ourselves where we stand on the important issues. Nothing should replace real conviction and seeking God for ourselves. Each person has to search the scriptures for themselves. Know what you believe or don't believe. Base your belief on what the scripture is saying, not what someone else is saying. I am convinced that holiness is required of each believer and that there is a solid foundation of scriptures in the Bible to support gender distinction and modesty in dress. However, in my time away, I discovered apostolics who parroted the scriptures they evidently heard from someone else, but which sometimes really didn't apply. When questioned, they could not provide any basis other than "that's just what we believe."

This experience really showed me how important it was to know the Word for myself. All too often I was speaking to "new generation" apostolics who also speak in tongues and who were baptized in Jesus name, but who refuse to set boundaries on how they dressed. In this environment, it is easy to be confused and to push personal conviction aside to follow those who appear more enlightened. My mistake was in forgetting what God had personally revealed to me, and in forgetting about Romans 3:4 (God is always right). In the meantime, I fought conviction, and tried my best to fit in with everyone else. My journey from here to there and back again has left me with a clear unequivocal understanding that clothing standards are about holiness. Holiness is still very relevant and important for the church today.

True holiness is on the inside. No amount of dressing right or acting right can substitute for what is needed on the inside. But true holiness on the inside must be reflected on the outside. A cake that is done on the inside must be done on the outside also, or else there is still some baking that needs to be done. God wants us to reflect holiness in our lifestyles, our thoughts, *and* our clothing choices.

When I eventually surrendered to God, the freedom that it brought to my life is almost unbelievable. It is a beautiful thing to surrender to the will of God. My only regret is that I didn't surrender sooner, but God deals with us individually. Like any parent, our heavenly Father knows how to bring each of us full circle if we are willing to let Him have His way. I thank God that although I walked away from holiness standards, His love and mercy brought me back again.

Thank you for taking the time to read
*Been There And Back Again.*

Sylvia Brown
P.O. Box 4424
South Bend, Indiana 46634
bookbeenthereandback@gmail.com

www.ingramcontent.com/pod-product-compliance
Ingram Content Group UK Ltd.
Pitfield, Milton Keynes, MK11 3LW, UK
UKHW041923190726
13854UKWH00003B/1414